R AMAZING!™

We find the amazing in the ordinary everyday with lists, polls and quizzes. Helping us to appreciate, in fun and quirky ways, the world in which we live.

Creating interactive content, R Amazing! is a safe place to explore different topics and share your views.

It is ok to disagree with us regarding who or what we think is amazing! We share our thoughts on our website and in our books to enable debate and discussion.

We encourage the expression of opinions in an appropriate way with an understanding that it is ok for people to have differing views.

R Amazing! debates should be conducted politely and respectfully, ending with an agreement and common ground, even if that is to agree to disagree.

www.r-amazing.com

Horses R Amazing!
Mark 'Markus' Baker & Adam Galvin

Published by R-and-Q.com.
Copyright © 2020 R-and-Q.com

All rights reserved.
ISBN: 978-1-9161450-8-5

HORSES

R Amazing!™

www.r-amazing.com/horses/

Adam Galvin and Markus Baker
Creators of R Amazing!

"The essential joy of being with horses is that it brings us in contact with the rare elements of grace, beauty, spirit and freedom."

Sharon Ralls Lemon

"

A pony is a
childhood dream...

...*A horse is an adulthood treasure.*

Rebecca Carroll

Horse Boy

When Rupert and Kirstin Isaacson discovered their two-year-old son Rowan was autistic they were unsure what life may hold. They could never have guessed the adventure it would lead them on.

Rowan grew more and more isolated and began to have major seizures. The Isaacson's tried many different treatments and were beginning to run out of options and hope. This all changed when Rowan discovered horses. Watching Rowan's first interaction with a horse, his parents were amazed at the connection the two of them had.

Researching the history of horses on the plains and mountains of Mongolia and discovering the healing powers of the Shamans. The Isaacson's risked everything for their son by uprooting their life and stability to make a horseback trip to find a cure for Rowan.

> *In a world that's changing really quickly, the only strategy that is guaranteed to fail is not taking risks.*
> Mark Zuckerberg

Seabiscuit

Overcoming his smaller stature and not winning his first 17 races, Seabiscuit went on to become one of the greatest racehorses of all time.

Seabiscuit's winning ways began when he was paired with the jockey Red Pollard. Unlocking Seabiscuit's winning mentality the victories continued even when Pollock become injured.

When Seabiscuit joined Red on the injury sideline, many felt the pair would never race again. However, overcoming adversity the pair both recovered to win races once again.

Coming together is a beginning.
Keeping together is progress.
Working together is success.
Henry Ford

DID YOU KNOW?

A horse's age can be estimated by its teeth using its length, grooves and angle.

There are many wonderful places in the world, but one of my favourite places is on the back of my horse.

Rolf Kopfle

Understanding Emotions

Having been shown photos of people with either a happy or angry expression, the reaction of 21 different horses were examined when they met the people in the photos in real life.

A few hours after seeing the original photo, the person would approach the horse with a neutral expression. The horses would remember the humans and their feelings by responding better to those that had been smiling in the photos.

Will you remember to smile the next time you introduce yourself to a horse?

A simple smile. That's the start of opening your heart and being compassionate to others.
Dalai Lama

Happier Horses

Born in 1935, Monty Roberts is a world-renowned horse trainer, who was inspired to find a kinder way to train horses after witnessing his father's traditional methods of domesticating a horse. Unfortunately, these ways were aggressive and brutal. Monty didn't like this and discovered his own way by using his body language, listening and responding to the horse's behavioural feedback. His methods are much kinder and so impressive even Queen Elizabeth II requested lessons from Monty.

Understanding that violence and aggression was not the best way to teach, many people resonated with Monty's kind and gentle techniques. Methods that have created many happier domesticated horses.

How do you best learn? Shouting and being hit or by kindness, gentleness and compassion?

"Kindness is the language which the deaf can hear and the blind can see."
Mark Twain

The world is best viewed through the ears of a horse.

Unknown

DID YOU KNOW?

Horses have the largest eyes of any land mammal. With 350 degrees vision that has only two blind spots, the first is in front and the second is directly behind them.

Source: https://www.horseandhound.co.uk/features/horse-facts-653825

Equine Assisted Therapy

Stroking, brushing, walking and mucking out specially trained horses are some of the activities that can help people to improve their physical and mental health.

A connection between a person and horse can help develop a calmness that allows the person to engage with nature. These naturally loving animals help humans to expand their trust, respect, communication skills and confidence into their everyday lives.

We will never have to tell our horse that we are sad, happy, confident, angry, or relaxed. He already knows - long before we do.

Marijke de Jong

World War 1

During World War 1 farms and country estates were requested to give their horses to the war effort.

Along with the battles on horseback by the cavalry, larger horses helped to deliver food and weapons to the soldiers.

After the war, six surviving war horses pulled the carriage of the Unknown Warrior to the last resting place at Westminster Abbey, London.

In this conflict alone, it is believed that an astounding 8 million horses were killed from shellfire, appalling conditions and being used to feed starving humans. How do you feel about the many sacrifices horses have made for humans?

> *They fight a war and they don't know what for. Isn't that crazy?*
> Michael Morpurgo, War Horse

DID YOU KNOW?

Horses are herbivores and only eat plant based foods.

> *At its finest, rider and horse are joined not by tack, but by trust. Each is totally reliant upon the other. Each is the selfless guardian of the other's very well-being.*
>
> Unknown

Rescue Horses

Horses that have been poorly treated are sometimes in need of being rescued by humans to ensure they have a better life going forward.

Animal rescue organisations have found horses that have been physically and mentally abused, starved, abandoned and living in horrible conditions.

With love, kindness and compassion most rescue horses go on to live happy healthy lives in much nicer environments. This is a testament to the connection between humans and horses.

After all the ways horses have helped us throughout history, do you think it is right that any horse is treated poorly? What do you think should happen to people who mistreat horses?

Saving just one horse will not change the world, but surely it will change the world for that one horse.

Unknown

Wild Horses

In the 1960s the Przewalski's Horse, named after the Russian explorer N. M. Przewalski, became extinct in the wild, it was the last wild horse to ever exist.

All horses that we now call wild are in fact feral horses who were once domesticated but reintroduced to their natural habitat to live as untamed wanderers living off the land. This includes the mustang in America, the brumby in Australia and many others including the Przewalski's Horse which was reintroduced in the 1980s to once again roam the plains of Mongolia.

> *Horse sense is the thing a horse has which keeps it from betting on people.*
> W.C. Fields

"

A man on a horse is spiritually, as well as physically, bigger than a man on foot.

John Steinbeck

DID YOU KNOW?

A horses height is measured in "hands." One hand is equal to four inches. The smallest horse on record was a miniature horse called Thumbelina who was just 4.2 hands tall, that is 43 centimetres or 17 inches tall!

Sleeping Horses

In a 24 hour period, a horse requires around 3 hours sleep.

A horse can sleep either lying down or standing up. This is because as a large animal a horse laying down for a long period of time can restrict their blood flow and cause damage to their internal organs.

For the few minutes each day that a horse is in deep sleep, they will need to lay down, deep sleep can be recognised when the horse moves their legs and may also be a sign that it is dreaming.

How do you think you would cope if you slept for just 3 hours a night?

A well spent day
brings happy sleep.
Leonardo da Vinci

Police Horses

All over the world horses are used to help with law enforcement. You may see trained police officers riding horses at sports events, protests and to protect important people. Mounted police are great at controlling large groups of people because of the horses' size and visibility. Being elevated above the masses gives police officers a great view and understanding of the whole situation they are policing, enabling them to protect and react to situations quickly and efficiently.

The training to become a police horse is very selective. Only 10% of the horses which start the training program are able to complete it. These are special horses because they are smart, have learnt how to overcome their fears and can deal with loud noises, crowds and being bumped into.

> *Avoiding danger is no safer in the long run than outright exposure. The fearful are caught as often as the bold.*
> Helen Keller

DID YOU KNOW?

Horses can rotate their ears 180 degrees and have 16 muscles in each ear compared to the 6 in a human ear.

Source: https://metro.co.uk/2016/04/19/15-things-you-probably-didnt-know-about-horses-5767687/

A horse doesn't care how much you know until he knows how much you care. Put your hand on your horse and your heart in your hand.

Pat Parelli

Shire Horses

A big horse with stamina and the strength to pull heavyweights, the Shire Horse has been used as a working horse to help humans complete their jobs more effectively.

Before tractors and powerful vehicles like lorries and buses, Shire Horses were used for farm work like ploughing, towing barges in the canals and as a cart-horse to deliver important items, like coal, beer and people, to their destination.

The largest horse ever was a Shire Horse named Sampson who was born in England. He measured an amazing 21.2 and a half hands. Using the formula mentioned earlier in this book, can you work out how tall Sampson was in centimetres and inches?

"

The Shire Horse – A magnificent animal. Tall, gentle, noble and immensely strong – loved by many.
The Shire Horse Society

Courage is being scared to death but saddling up anyway.

John Wayne

DID YOU KNOW?

As social animals, Horses will get lonely if left on their own, and they will grieve if a companion dies.

Source: http://www.theequinest.com/random-horse-facts/

My picture of the most amazing horse in the world!

The most amazing horse in the world is

. . . .

I love it when this amazing horse...

....

....

....

....

....

....

This horse is amazing because...

....

....

....

....

MORE BOOKS BY R&Q

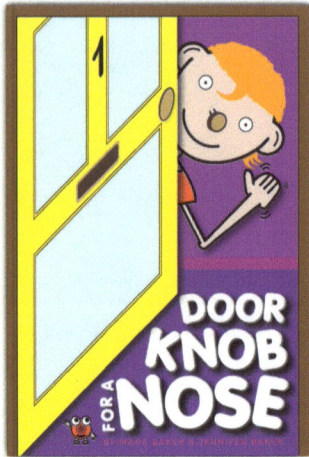

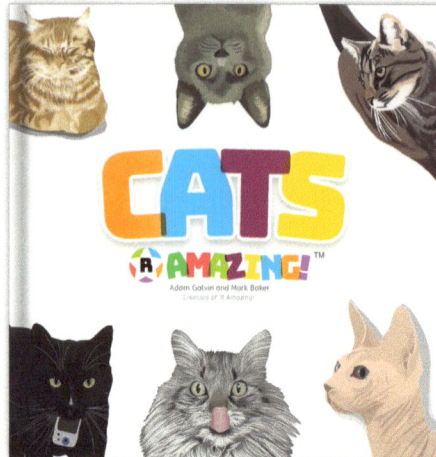

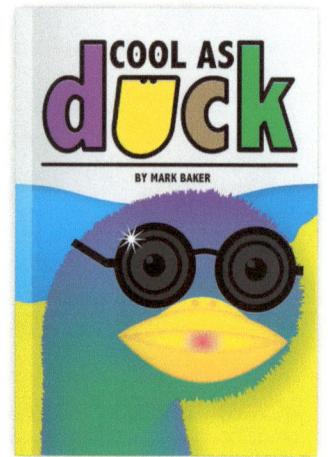

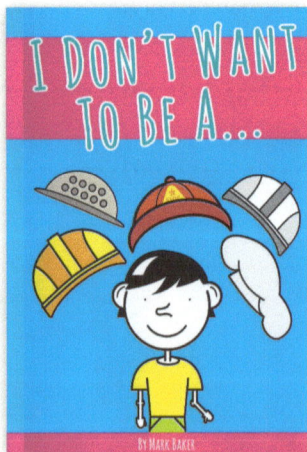

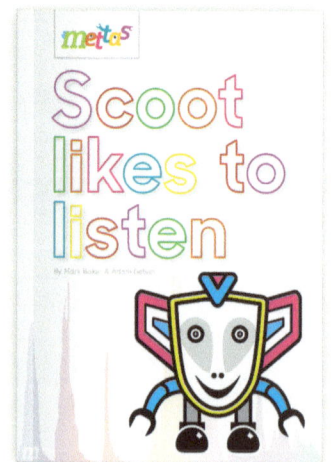

DOOR KNOB FOR A NOSE

CATS R AMAZING!
Adam Galvin and Mark Baker

COOL AS duck
BY MARK BAKER

I DON'T WANT TO BE A...
By Mark Baker

THIS BOOK NEVER ENDS...
...it keeps looping round and round until somebody says "PLEASE STOP READING NOW!"
Who is going to give up first? The grown up or the child because...
By Mark Baker

mettos
Scoot likes to listen

www.ingramcontent.com/pod-product-compliance
Lightning Source LLC
Chambersburg PA
CBHW060832270326
41933CB00002B/56

9 781916 145085